Easy Cajun Cookbook

Authentic Cajun and Creole Cooking

By
Chef Maggie Chow
Copyright © 2015 by Saxonberg Associates
All rights reserved

Published by
BookSumo, a division of Saxonberg Associates
http://www.booksumo.com/

INTRODUCTION

Welcome to *The Effortless Chef Series*! Thank you for taking the time to download the *Easy Cajun Cookbook*. Come take a journey with me into the delights of easy cooking. The point of this cookbook and all my cookbooks is to exemplify the effortless nature of cooking simply.

In this book we focus on Cajun. You will find that even though the recipes are simple, the taste of the dishes is quite amazing.

So will you join me in an adventure of simple cooking? If the answer is yes (and I hope it is) please consult the table of contents to find the dishes you are most interested in. Once you are ready jump right in and start cooking.

— Chef Maggie Chow

TABLE OF CONTENTS

Introduction 2

Table of Contents 3

Any Issues? Contact Me 7

Legal Notes 8

Common Abbreviations 9

Chapter 1: Easy Cajun Recipes 10

    Creole Spice Mix 10

    Cajun Spice 12

    Thibodeaux Gumbo 14

    Cajun Pasta 18

    Louisiana Boudin 21

    Cajun Pork 24

    Cajun Pinto Beans 27

    Cajun Turkey 30

Cajun Pie	33
Cajun Prawns	36
Maggie's Classical Creole Chicken	38
Louisiana Paella	40
Baton Rouge Gravy	42
Cajun Linguine	44
Creole Cake	47
Creole Meatloaf	50
Crawfish and Shrimp	53
Cajun Bisque	56
Cajun Gumbo II	59
Creole Peppers	61
Creole Soup	64
Hannah's Jambalaya	66
Cajun Burger	69
Cajun Pulled Pork	71
Cajun Pretzel	73

Cajun Breakfast 75

Creole Corn 77

Creole Fried Snapper 79

Creole Fried Catfish 81

Louisiana Chowder 83

French Quarter Mushrooms 85

Cajun Burger II 87

Bayou Blue Salad 89

Mardi-Gras Potatoes 91

Creole Fries 93

Cajun Mushrooms and Broccoli 95

Creole Cabbage 97

Creole Cauliflower 99

Bayou Andouille Rice 101

Crossroads Beef 103

Cajun County Stuffing 105

Louisiana Popcorn 107

Cajun Country Dough 109

Greater New Orleans Stew 112

Southern Louisiana Vegetable Medley (Maque Choux) 115

Cajun Seeds 118

Cajun Lasagna 120

Muffuletta (Louisiana Sandwich) 123

Creole Pasta II 126

Po' Boy 129

Jambalaya V 132

Bourbon Chicken II 134

THANKS FOR READING! NOW LET'S TRY SOME **SUSHI** AND **DUMP DINNERS**.. 137

Come On 139

Let's Be Friends :) 139

Can I Ask A Favour? 140

Interested in Other Easy Cookbooks? 141

ANY ISSUES? CONTACT ME

If you find that something important to you is missing from this book please contact me at maggie@booksumo.com.

I will try my best to re-publish a revised copy taking your feedback into consideration and let you know when the book has been revised with you in mind.

:)

— Chef Maggie Chow

LEGAL NOTES

ALL RIGHTS RESERVED. NO PART OF THIS BOOK MAY BE REPRODUCED OR TRANSMITTED IN ANY FORM OR BY ANY MEANS. PHOTOCOPYING, POSTING ONLINE, AND / OR DIGITAL COPYING IS STRICTLY PROHIBITED UNLESS WRITTEN PERMISSION IS GRANTED BY THE BOOK'S PUBLISHING COMPANY. LIMITED USE OF THE BOOK'S TEXT IS PERMITTED FOR USE IN REVIEWS WRITTEN FOR THE PUBLIC AND/OR PUBLIC DOMAIN.

Common Abbreviations

cup(s)	C.
tablespoon	tbsp
teaspoon	tsp
ounce	oz.
pound	lb

*All units used are standard American measurements

Chapter 1: Easy Cajun Recipes

Creole Spice Mix

Ingredients

- 2 tbsps onion powder
- 2 tbsps garlic powder
- 2 tbsps dried oregano
- 2 tbsps dried basil
- 1 tbsp dried thyme
- 1 tbsp black pepper
- 1 tbsp white pepper
- 1 tbsp cayenne pepper
- 5 tbsps paprika
- 3 tbsps salt

Directions

- Get a bowl, combine: salt, onion powder, paprika, garlic powder, cayenne, oregano, white pepper, thyme, black pepper, and basil.
- Stir the spices evenly then place them in a shaker or spice container.
- Enjoy.

Amount per serving (20 total)

Timing Information:

Preparation	
Cooking	5 m
Total Time	5 m

Nutritional Information:

Calories	16 kcal
Fat	< 0.4 g
Carbohydrates	< 3.4g
Protein	0.7 g
Cholesterol	0 mg
Sodium	1048 mg

* Percent Daily Values are based on a 2,000 calorie diet.

CAJUN SPICE

Ingredients

- 2 tsps salt
- 2 tsps garlic powder
- 2 1/2 tsps paprika
- 1 tsp ground black pepper
- 1 tsp onion powder
- 1 tsp cayenne pepper
- 1 1/4 tsps dried oregano
- 1 1/4 tsps dried thyme
- 1/2 tsp red pepper flakes

Directions

- Get a bowl, combine: pepper flakes, thyme, oregano, cayenne, onion powder, black pepper, paprika, garlic powder, and salt.
- Stir the spice mix evenly then place everything into a shaker or spice container.
- Enjoy.

Amount per serving (12 total)

Timing Information:

Preparation	
Cooking	5 m
Total Time	5 m

Nutritional Information:

Calories	6 kcal
Fat	< 0.1 g
Carbohydrates	< 1.2g
Protein	< 0.2 g
Cholesterol	< 0 mg
Sodium	388 mg

* Percent Daily Values are based on a 2,000 calorie diet.

THIBODEAUX GUMBO

Ingredients

- 1 C. all-purpose flour
- 3/4 C. bacon drippings
- 1 C. coarsely chopped celery
- 1 large onion, coarsely chopped
- 1 large green bell pepper, coarsely chopped
- 2 cloves garlic, diced
- 1 lb andouille sausage, sliced
- 3 quarts water
- 6 cubes beef bouillon
- 1 tbsp white sugar
- salt to taste
- 2 tbsps hot pepper sauce
- 1/2 tsp Cajun seasoning blend
- 4 bay leaves
- 1/2 tsp dried thyme leaves
- 1 (14.5 oz.) can stewed tomatoes
- 1 (6 oz.) can tomato sauce
- 2 tsps gumbo file powder
- 2 tbsps bacon drippings
- 2 (10 oz.) packages frozen cut okra, thawed
- 2 tbsps distilled white vinegar
- 1 lb lump crabmeat
- 3 lbs uncooked medium shrimp, peeled and deveined
- 2 tbsps Worcestershire sauce
- 2 tsps gumbo file powder

Directions

- Get a large pot and begin to heat and stir 3/4 C. of bacon drippings with flour.
- Heat the mix with a medium to low level of heat and form a roux.
- Once the roux becomes a brown color you are finished.
- Cooking the roux should take about 24 mins. Make sure you stir consistently during this time. Once the roux is done shut the heat.
- Now chop the following with a food processor: garlic, celery, bell peppers, and onions.
- Add these chopped veggies to the roux and also add in the sausage.
- Get the mix simmering with a low level of heat and let everything cook for 12 mins.
- Now shut the heat again.
- Get a separate pot and begin to boil your bouillon and water until the bouillon is dissolved.
- Once the bouillon is fully incorporated add in the roux to the bouillon mix.
- Set the heat to low then add in: the tomato sauce, sugar, stewed tomatoes, salt, thyme, hot sauce, bay leaves, and Cajun spice.
- Stir the mix until it is smooth and let the gumbo simmer for 60 mins.
- When 20 mins of cooking time is left add in 2 tsps of gumbo powder.
- At the same time begin to stir fry your okra in 2 tbsps of bacon drippings for 20 mins then add the okra to the gumbo.
- Stir the gumbo then add in the Worcestershire, shrimp, and crab.

- Stir the meat into the gumbo and let everything cook for 50 more mins.
- Then add in 2 more tsps of gumbo powder and mix everything.
- Enjoy.

Amount per serving (20 total)

Timing Information:

Preparation	1 h
Cooking	2 h 40 m
Total Time	3 h 40 m

Nutritional Information:

Calories	296 kcal
Fat	17.9 g
Carbohydrates	12.1g
Protein	20.9 g
Cholesterol	144 mg
Sodium	855 mg

* Percent Daily Values are based on a 2,000 calorie diet.

Cajun Pasta

Ingredients

- 1/2 C. vegetable oil
- 8 oz. tomato sauce
- 1 C. water
- 1/4 tsp dried basil
- 1 tsp ground black pepper
- 1 tsp crushed red pepper flakes
- 1 tsp salt
- 1 lb small shrimp, peeled and deveined
- 1 green bell pepper, chopped
- 1 red bell pepper, chopped
- 1/2 onion, chopped
- 3 cloves garlic, diced
- 2 tsps cornstarch
- 1 fluid oz. cold water
- 12 oz. spaghetti
- 8 green onions, diced

Directions

- In a pot combine the following: 1/2 tsp salt, 4 oz. oil, 1/2 tsp pepper flakes, tomato sauce, 1/2 tsp black pepper, 10 oz. of water, and basil.
- Stir the mix and get everything boiling.
- Once the mix is boiling set the heat to low.
- Get a bowl, combine: 1/2 tsp pepper flakes, 1/2 tsp salt, 1/2 tsp black pepper, and the shrimp.

- Evenly coat the shrimp with the spices then place everything to the side.
- In a separate pot begin to stir fry your bell peppers, garlic, and onions in 1 oz. of oil for 7 mins then add these veggies to the tomato sauce.
- Let the veggies cook for 5 mins with a medium level of heat then set the heat to low again and cook everything for 30 mins.
- Stir the mix every 10 mins.
- After 20 mins of simmering the tomato sauce and veggies add in the shrimp and continue simmering the mix for 10 more mins with a medium level of heat to fully cook the shrimp.
- Get a bowl, combine: 1 oz. water and cornstarch.
- Stir the mix until it is smooth then combine it with the simmering tomato sauce mix when 5 mins of time is left.
- Now get your pasta boiling in water and salt for 9 mins, in a separate pot then remove all the liquids.
- Divide your pasta into bowls for serving.
- Then liberally top each serving with tomato sauce and some green onions.
- Enjoy.

Amount per serving (5 total)

Timing Information:

Preparation	20 m
Cooking	1 h 30 m
Total Time	2 h

Nutritional Information:

Calories	585 kcal
Fat	25 g
Carbohydrates	61g
Protein	29 g
Cholesterol	138 mg
Sodium	845 mg

* Percent Daily Values are based on a 2,000 calorie diet.

Louisiana Boudin

Ingredients

- 2 1/2 lbs boneless pork shoulder, cubed
- 1 lb pork liver, cut into pieces
- 4 C. water
- 2 C. uncooked white rice
- 4 C. water
- 1 1/4 C. green onions, chopped
- 1 C. chopped onion
- 1/2 C. diced celery
- 1 red bell pepper, chopped
- 1 C. chopped fresh parsley
- 2 tbsps finely chopped cilantro
- 1 tsp diced garlic
- 4 tsps salt
- 2 1/2 tsps cayenne pepper
- 1 1/2 tsps ground black pepper
- 1/2 tsp red pepper flakes
- 4 feet 1 1/2 inch diameter hog casings, cleaned thoroughly

Directions

- Get the following boiling in a large pot: 4 C. water, liver, and pork shoulder.
- Once the mix is boiling set the heat to a low / medium level, place a lid on the pot, and cook everything for 90 mins.
- Get your rice boiling in 4 C. of water.

- Once the mix is boiling, set the heat to low, place a lid on the pot, and cook the rice for 22 mins.
- Remove the pork from the pot and place it to the side to lose its heat.
- Now add in the following to simmering mix: pepper flakes, green onions, black pepper, chopped onions, cayenne, celery, salt, bell pepper, garlic, cilantro, and parsley.
- Let this mix simmer until the onions are soft.
- As the mix is cooking grind your pork then add it to the mix.
- Heat and stir the mix for 12 mins. Then add the cooked rice and shut the heat.
- Stuff the mix into the casing once it is cool enough to handle then perforate each sausage with a needle, a few times, all over.
- Get a saucepan of water and salt boiling then set the heat to a medium level and cook the sausages for 7 mins.
- Enjoy.

Amount per serving (18 total)

Timing Information:

Preparation	30 m
Cooking	2 h
Total Time	3 h 30 m

Nutritional Information:

Calories	188 kcal
Fat	6.6 g
Carbohydrates	20g
Protein	11.2 g
Cholesterol	64 mg
Sodium	551 mg

* Percent Daily Values are based on a 2,000 calorie diet.

Cajun Pork

Ingredients

- 2 tbsps butter
- 1/2 tsp cayenne pepper
- 1 tsp dried oregano
- 1/2 tsp ground black pepper
- 1/2 tsp dried thyme
- 1/2 tsp ground mustard
- 2 cloves garlic, diced
- 1 (4 lb) pork loin roast
- salt and pepper to taste
- 1 tbsp olive oil
- 2 carrot, cut into 1/2 inch pieces
- 1 red bell pepper, cut into 1/2 inch pieces
- 1 stalk celery, cut into 1/2 inch pieces
- 1 large onion, cut into 1/2-inch pieces
- 3 tbsps all-purpose flour
- 1/2 C. chicken broth

Directions

- Set your oven to 300 degrees before doing anything else.
- Stir fry the garlic, cayenne, mustard, oregano, thyme, and pepper in butter for 2 mins.
- Cut some incisions into the fat of the meat then fill the incisions with the spice mix.
- Now coat the meat all over with the remaining spice mix.

- Top the meat with some pepper and salt then begin to heat the olive oil in a roasting pan with a medium level of heat.
- Place the meat in the pan then layer the following around it: onion, carrots, celery, and red pepper.
- Top the veggies with some pepper and salt then put everything in the oven for 2 hrs.
- Turn up the temperature to 425 degrees and continue roasting everything for 20 more mins.
- Place the meat to the side and slice it once it has cooled.
- As the meat cools place the pan on the stove with a medium level of heat and begin to stir flour into the liquids in the pan for 4 mins.
- Add in the chicken stock and continue stirring and heating everything for 7 more mins.
- Run the liquid through a strainer and top the pork with it.
- Enjoy.

Amount per serving (8 total)

Timing Information:

Preparation	15 m
Cooking	2 h 10 m
Total Time	2 h 25 m

Nutritional Information:

Calories	409 kcal
Fat	24.5 g
Carbohydrates	7.4g
Protein	37.5 g
Cholesterol	118 mg
Sodium	178 mg

* Percent Daily Values are based on a 2,000 calorie diet.

Cajun Pinto Beans

Ingredients

- 1 lb dried pinto beans
- 3 tbsps bacon grease
- 1/4 C. chopped salt pork
- 1 1/2 C. chopped yellow onion
- 3/4 C. chopped celery
- 3/4 C. chopped green bell pepper
- 1/2 tsp freshly ground black pepper
- 1 pinch chipotle chile powder
- 1/2 lb smoked sausage, split in half and cut into 1-inch pieces
- 3 bay leaves
- 2 tbsps chopped fresh parsley
- 2 tsps chopped fresh thyme
- 3 tbsps chopped garlic
- water as needed

Directions

- Let your beans sit submerged in water for 30 mins. Then remove the liquid and run the beans under some fresh cold water.
- Begin to stir fry your salt pork for 2 mins in bacon drippings, in a big pot, then stir in: the chipotle powder, onion, black pepper, celery, and bell peppers.
- Continue to stir fry the mix for 5 mins then add in the thyme, smoked sausage, parsley, and bay leaves.

- Let everything continue to fry for 5 more mins then add in the garlic and cook everything for 2 more mins.
- Add the beans to the mix and submerge everything in just enough water to cover it.
- Get the mix boiling then once everything is boiling shut the heat and place the mix into the crock pot of a slow cooker.
- Cook the mix for 60 mins with a high level of heat, set the heat to low, and continue cooking everything for 6 more hrs.
- Remove 1/4 of the beans into a bowl and mash them then add the beans back into the mix and continue cooking everything for 17 more mins.
- Enjoy.

Amount per serving (8 total)

Timing Information:

Preparation	20 m
Cooking	7 h 10 m
Total Time	7 h 45 m

Nutritional Information:

Calories	430 kcal
Fat	20.7 g
Carbohydrates	41.2g
Protein	19.6 g
Cholesterol	30 mg
Sodium	555 mg

* Percent Daily Values are based on a 2,000 calorie diet.

Cajun Turkey

Ingredients

- 2 C. butter
- 1/4 C. onion juice
- 1/4 C. garlic juice
- 1/4 C. Louisiana-style hot sauce
- 1/4 C. Worcestershire sauce
- 2 tbsps ground black pepper
- 1 tsp cayenne pepper
- 3 gallons peanut oil for frying, or as needed
- 1 (12 lb) whole turkey, neck and giblets removed

Directions

- Begin to stir fry the following, in butter, in a large pot: cayenne, onion juice, black pepper, garlic juice, Worcestershire, and hot sauce.
- Heat and stir the mix until it is smooth for a few mins then use a baster to coat your turkey with the mix and also add some of the mix inside the turkey.
- Place the meat into a bowl and place a covering of plastic over the bowl. Then put everything in the fridge.
- To fry the turkey properly, you will need to first determine the proper amount of oil.

- To do this easily, place the turkey in a big pot then add in enough oil to submerge it.
- Now place the turkey to the side and get the oil hot to 365 degrees before continuing.
- Place your turkey into the oil carefully.
- The best way to do this is with a turkey hanger that you get with a turkey fryer.
- Let the meat fry for 40 mins or 4 mins for each lb of meat.
- Remove the meat from the oil and let as much of the oil drain out as possible then place the turkey to the side for at least 30 mins to let it lose its heat.
- Enjoy.

Amount per serving (12 total)

Timing Information:

Preparation	30 m
Cooking	45 m
Total Time	1 h 15 m

Nutritional Information:

Calories	1036 kcal
Fat	70.9 g
Carbohydrates	12.8g
Protein	< 91.2 g
Cholesterol	1346 mg
Sodium	1682 mg

* Percent Daily Values are based on a 2,000 calorie diet.

Cajun Pie

Ingredients

- 1 deep dish pastry for double crust
- 2 tbsps olive oil
- 3 skinless, boneless chicken breast halves, cut into bite size pieces
- salt and ground black pepper to taste
- 1 (8 oz.) package portobello mushrooms, chopped
- 1 (10.75 oz.) can cream of chicken soup
- 1 (10.75 oz.) can cream of mushroom soup
- 1/2 C. chicken broth
- 1 (8 oz.) package cream cheese, softened
- 1/2 (14.5 oz.) can chopped tomatoes, drained
- 3 C. frozen mixed vegetables, thawed
- 1/4 tsp crushed red pepper flakes (optional)

Directions

- Coat a pie pan with nonstick spray then set your oven to 375 degrees before doing anything else.
- Begin to fry your chicken in olive oil, in a frying pan, until it is fully done for 9 mins then combine in the mushrooms and cook everything until they are soft.

- Now add the cream of mushroom and cream chicken, tomatoes, cream cheese, and broth to the mix.
- Combine the mix until it is smooth then add in the pepper flakes and the mixed veggies.
- Stir everything again and get the mix simmering.
- Enter the mix into your pie and place the top part of the crust over the pie.
- Seal the edges then perforate the top of your pie with a few holes.
- Place a covering of foil over the pie and cook everything in the oven for 55 mins.
- Enjoy.

Amount per serving (6 total)

Timing Information:

Preparation	15 m
Cooking	1 h
Total Time	1 h 15 m

Nutritional Information:

Calories	655 kcal
Fat	40.4 g
Carbohydrates	49.8g
Protein	23.5 g
Cholesterol	79 mg
Sodium	996 mg

* Percent Daily Values are based on a 2,000 calorie diet.

Cajun Prawns

Ingredients

- 1 tsp paprika
- 3/4 tsp dried thyme
- 3/4 tsp dried oregano
- 1/4 tsp garlic powder
- 1/4 tsp salt
- 1/4 tsp ground black pepper
- 1/4 tsp cayenne pepper, or more to taste
- 1 1/2 lbs large shrimp, peeled and deveined
- 1 tbsp vegetable oil

Directions

- Get a bowl, combine: cayenne, paprika, pepper, thyme, salt, garlic powder, and oregano.
- Stir the mix then add in the shrimp and stir everything again to evenly coat the pieces of shrimp.
- Begin to stir fry the shrimp in the veggie oil until the pieces are completely done for 6 mins.
- Enjoy.

Amount per serving (4 total)

Timing Information:

Preparation	5 m
Cooking	5 m
Total Time	10 m

Nutritional Information:

Calories	166 kcal
Fat	5 g
Carbohydrates	0.9g
Protein	< 28 g
Cholesterol	259 mg
Sodium	443 mg

* Percent Daily Values are based on a 2,000 calorie diet.

Maggie's Classical Creole Chicken

Ingredients

- 2 C. vegetable oil
- 2 tbsps Cajun seasoning
- 2 tbsps dried Italian-style seasoning
- garlic powder to taste
- 2 tbsps lemon pepper
- 10 skinless, boneless chicken breast halves, flattened

Directions

- Get a bowl, combine: lemon pepper, oil, garlic powder, Cajun spice, and Italian seasoning.
- Stir the mix until it is smooth then add in the chicken and evenly coat the pieces of meat with the mix.
- Place a covering of plastic on the bowl and put everything in the fridge for 40 mins.
- Now get an outdoor grill hot and coat the grate with oil.
- Cook the chicken on the grill for 7 mins each side until the meat is fully done.
- Enjoy.

Amount per serving (10 total)

Timing Information:

Preparation	15 m
Cooking	15 m
Total Time	1 h

Nutritional Information:

Calories	536 kcal
Fat	47.8 g
Carbohydrates	1.8g
Protein	< 24.8 g
Cholesterol	67 mg
Sodium	620 mg

* Percent Daily Values are based on a 2,000 calorie diet.

Louisiana Paella

Ingredients

- 2 tbsps olive oil
- 4 chicken leg quarters
- 2 (8 oz.) packages dirty rice mix
- 5 C. water
- 2 lbs whole cooked crawfish, peeled
- 3/4 medium shrimp, peeled and deveined
- 1/2 lb andouille sausage, sliced into rounds
- 2 C. sliced mushrooms
- 1 large green bell pepper, chopped
- 1 large sweet onion, chopped
- 3 cloves garlic, diced

Directions

- Get your oil hot in a big pot then add in the chicken and brown the meat all over.
- Now add the water and the rice.
- Stir the mix then add in the garlic, crawfish, onion, shrimp, bell peppers, mushrooms, and sausage.
- Get everything boiling while stirring.
- Once the mix is boiling, place a lid on the pot, set the heat to low, and let the paella cook for 35 mins. Enjoy.

Amount per serving (6 total)

Timing Information:

Preparation	30 m
Cooking	45 m
Total Time	1 h 15 m

Nutritional Information:

Calories	757 kcal
Fat	30.5 g
Carbohydrates	62.8g
Protein	54.6 g
Cholesterol	1277 mg
Sodium	1867 mg

* Percent Daily Values are based on a 2,000 calorie diet.

Baton Rouge Gravy

Ingredients

- 2 (4.5 oz.) cans chopped green chilies
- 1 1/2 tsps chicken bouillon granules
- 1 1/2 C. warm water, divided
- 1/4 C. all-purpose flour
- 1 tsp onion powder
- 1/8 tsp ground cayenne pepper, or to taste

Directions

- Begin to puree your chilies with a food processor.
- Get a large pot and get 1 C. of water and the bouillon boiling as well.
- Stir the mix until the bouillon is completely combined then add in the chilies.
- Get the mix boiling again then set the heat to a low level.
- Get a bowl, combine: flour and 1/2 C. of warm water. Once the mix is evenly combined it with the chili mix.
- Get everything boiling again, set the heat to medium, and cook everything for 6 mins.
- Now combine in the cayenne and onion powder.
- Enjoy.

Amount per serving (8 total)

Timing Information:

Preparation	5 m
Cooking	10 m
Total Time	15 m

Nutritional Information:

Calories	23 kcal
Fat	0.1 g
Carbohydrates	< 4.9g
Protein	0.8 g
Cholesterol	< 1 mg
Sodium	< 447 mg

* Percent Daily Values are based on a 2,000 calorie diet.

Cajun Linguine

Ingredients

- 4 oz. linguine pasta
- 2 skinless, boneless chicken breast halves
- 2 tsps Cajun seasoning
- 2 tbsps butter
- 1 red bell pepper, sliced
- 1 green bell pepper, sliced
- 4 fresh mushrooms, sliced
- 1 green onion, chopped
- 1 C. heavy cream
- 1/4 tsp dried basil
- 1/4 tsp lemon pepper
- 1/4 tsp salt
- 1/8 tsp garlic powder
- 1/8 tsp ground black pepper
- 1/4 C. grated Parmesan cheese

Directions

- Get your pasta boiling in water and salt for 9 mins then remove all the liquids.
- Get a bowl, combine: chicken and Cajun spice.
- Evenly coat the meat then stir fry the chicken in butter for 9 mins.
- Combine in the green onions, bell peppers, and mushrooms and continue to stir fry the mix for 4 mins then set the heat to low.

- Add in the black pepper, cream, garlic powder, basil, salt, and lemon pepper.
- Combine the spices into the mix evenly then add in the pasta and stir everything.
- Top the mix with the parmesan.
- Enjoy.

Amount per serving (2 total)

Timing Information:

Preparation	20 m
Cooking	20 m
Total Time	40 m

Nutritional Information:

Calories	935 kcal
Fat	61.7 g
Carbohydrates	54g
Protein	43.7 g
Cholesterol	271 mg
Sodium	1189 mg

* Percent Daily Values are based on a 2,000 calorie diet.

CREOLE CAKE

Ingredients

- 3 C. all-purpose flour
- 1 1/2 C. white sugar
- 2 tsps baking soda
- 1/4 tsp salt
- 2 eggs
- 1 (20 oz.) can crushed pineapple with juice

Topping:

- 3/4 C. white sugar
- 3/4 C. evaporated milk
- 1/2 C. margarine
- 1 C. chopped pecans
- 1 1/2 C. flaked coconut

Directions

- Coat a casserole dish with flour and oil then set your oven to 350 degrees before doing anything else.
- Get a bowl combine: baking soda, flour, salt, and 1.5 C. of sugar.
- Stir the mix then combine in the pineapple with liquid, and the eggs. Get an electric mixer and combine everything for 1 min with a low speed.
- Enter everything into the casserole dish then cook it all in the oven for 32 mins.

- At the same time get the following boiling: margarine, milk, and 3/4 C. of sugar.
- Let the mix cook for 3 mins while whisking everything together then add in the coconut and the pecans.
- Now shut the heat and top the cake with the coconut mix.
- Enjoy.

Amount per serving (12 total)

Timing Information:

Preparation	30 m
Cooking	1 h
Total Time	1 h 30 m

Nutritional Information:

Calories	492 kcal
Fat	19 g
Carbohydrates	76.5g
Protein	6.8 g
Cholesterol	36 mg
Sodium	402 mg

* Percent Daily Values are based on a 2,000 calorie diet.

Creole Meatloaf

Ingredients

- 2 bay leaves
- 1 tsp salt
- 1 tsp ground cayenne pepper
- 1 tsp ground black pepper
- 1/2 tsp ground white pepper
- 1/2 tsp ground cumin
- 1/2 tsp ground nutmeg
- 4 tbsps butter
- 3/4 C. chopped onion
- 1/2 C. chopped green bell pepper
- 1/4 C. chopped green onions
- 4 cloves garlic, diced
- 1 tbsp hot pepper sauce
- 1 tbsp Worcestershire sauce
- 1/2 C. evaporated milk
- 1/2 C. ketchup
- 1 1/2 lbs ground beef
- 1/2 lb andouille sausage, casings removed
- 2 eggs, beaten
- 1 C. dried bread crumbs

Directions

- Set your oven to 350 degrees doing anything else.
- Get a bowl combine: nutmeg, bay leaves, cumin, salt, white pepper, cayenne, and black pepper.
- Now begin to stir fry the following in butter for 7 mins: spice mix, onion, Worcestershire, bell pepper, hot sauce, garlic, and green onions.

- Add in the ketchup and the milk. Then stir the mix completely.
- Let everything continue to cook for 3 more mins. Then shut the heat.
- Layer your sausage and beef in a casserole dish then add in the bread crumbs, veggie mix, and eggs.
- Discard the bay leaves then stir everything completely with your hands.
- Shape the mix into a loaf then cook it in the oven for 30 mins.
- Set the heat to 400 degrees and continue cooking the loaf for 40 more mins.
- Enjoy.

Amount per serving (8 total)

Timing Information:

Preparation	20 m
Cooking	1 h
Total Time	1 h 20 m

Nutritional Information:

Calories	548 kcal
Fat	40.8 g
Carbohydrates	19.3g
Protein	25.7 g
Cholesterol	158 mg
Sodium	1184 mg

* Percent Daily Values are based on a 2,000 calorie diet.

Crawfish and Shrimp

Ingredients

- 1/3 C. vegetable oil
- 1/4 C. all-purpose flour
- 1 small green bell pepper, diced
- 1 medium onion, chopped
- 2 cloves garlic, diced
- 2 stalks celery, diced
- 2 fresh tomatoes, chopped
- 2 tbsps Louisiana-style hot sauce
- 1/3 tsp ground cayenne pepper
- 2 tbsps seafood seasoning
- 1/2 tsp ground black pepper
- 1 C. fish stock
- 1 lb crawfish tails
- 1 lb medium shrimp, peeled and deveined

Directions

- Stir fry some flour in a pan for 15 to 22 mins until its color becomes brown.
- Now add your bell peppers, onions, celery, and garlic.
- Continue cooking everything for 7 mins until it is tender.
- Then add in the seafood seasoning, fish stock, and tomatoes.

- Set your heat to the lowest level and let the contents lightly boil for 22 mins.
- Stir the mix every 2 to 4 mins.
- Finally add in some cayenne and hot sauce. Then the shrimp and crawfish.
- Let the fish simmer in the sauce for 13 mins.
- Enjoy.

Amount per serving (6 total)

Timing Information:

Preparation	20 m
Cooking	50 m
Total Time	1 h 10 m

Nutritional Information:

Calories	264 kcal
Fat	14 g
Carbohydrates	9g
Protein	24.9 g
Cholesterol	196 mg
Sodium	956 mg

* Percent Daily Values are based on a 2,000 calorie diet.

Cajun Bisque

Ingredients

- 3 tbsps butter
- 3 tbsps all-purpose flour
- 1 tbsp vegetable oil
- 1 large onion, chopped
- 1 tbsp diced garlic
- 1 large celery stalk, diced
- Cajun seasoning to taste
- 1 C. chicken broth
- 1 1/2 C. frozen corn kernels
- 1 bay leaf
- 2 C. milk
- 2 C. heavy cream
- 1 tsp liquid shrimp and crab boil seasoning
- 1 lb fresh lump crabmeat
- 1/4 C. chopped green onions
- 1/2 tsp Worcestershire sauce
- salt and black pepper to taste
- chopped green onions

Directions

- Heat and stir your flour and butter for 6 mins then shut the heat.
- Get a separate large pot and begin to stir fry your celery, garlic, and onion for 2 mins then combine in some Cajun spice.
- Stir the mix then add in the bay leaf, corn, and broth.
- Stir everything again.
- Now get the mix boiling, then add the crab boil, cream, and milk.

- Set the heat to low and let the mix gently cook for 9 mins.
- Begin to slowly add in the butter flour mix and combine the contents evenly.
- Keep cooking everything for 7 mins then add the Worcestershire, green onions, and crab meat.
- Add some pepper and salt.
- Enjoy.

Amount per serving (8 total)

Timing Information:

Preparation	20 m
Cooking	30 m
Total Time	50 m

Nutritional Information:

Calories	387 kcal
Fat	30.1 g
Carbohydrates	16.3g
Protein	14.8 g
Cholesterol	131 mg
Sodium	278 mg

* Percent Daily Values are based on a 2,000 calorie diet.

Cajun Gumbo II

Ingredients

- 1 C. vegetable oil
- 1 C. all-purpose flour
- 1 large onion, chopped
- 1 large green bell pepper, chopped
- 2 celery stalks, chopped
- 1 lb andouille or smoked sausage, sliced 1/4 inch thick
- 4 cloves garlic, diced
- salt and pepper to taste
- Creole seasoning to taste
- 6 C. chicken broth
- 1 bay leaf
- 1 rotisserie chicken, boned and shredded

Directions

- For 12 mins, stir fry, the flour and oil to make a brown roux.
- Make sure your roux does not have any black dots in it. If so, try again.
- Now add sausage, onions, celery, and bell pepper and cook the mix for 7 mins. Add in your garlic and let the contents cook for 6 more mins.
- Add the creole seasoning, pepper, broth, salt, and bay leaf.
- Get the broth boiling, set the heat to low, and let the mix lightly cook for 1 hour. Now stir in your chicken and cook the mix for 1 more hour. Try to stir the dish every 10 mins. Enjoy.

Amount per serving (10 total)

Timing Information:

Preparation	45 m
Cooking	2 h 30 m
Total Time	3 h 15 m

Nutritional Information:

Calories	478 kcal
Fat	39.4 g
Carbohydrates	14.3g
Protein	16 g
Cholesterol	56 mg
Sodium	1045 mg

* Percent Daily Values are based on a 2,000 calorie diet.

CREOLE PEPPERS

Ingredients

- 6 large green bell peppers
- 3 tbsps olive oil
- 1 onion, diced
- 2 cloves garlic, diced
- 1/2 tsp dried oregano
- 1 tbsp Creole seasoning
- black pepper to taste
- 3/4 lb shrimp, peeled and deveined
- 1 1/2 links of andouille sausage, diced
- 1 C. uncooked long-grain white rice
- 2 1/2 C. chicken broth
- 1 (8 oz.) can tomato sauce

Directions

- Coat a casserole dish with oil then set your oven to 325 degrees before doing anything else.
- Slice off the top portion of your peppers and remove the insides.
- Place the peppers in the boiling water for 4 mins then place them to the side inverted on some pepper towels.
- Begin to stir fry your onions, in olive oil, until they are see-through, then add in: the garlic, black pepper, creole spice, and oregano.
- Stir the mix, then add in the sausage and shrimp.

- Stir the mix again then fry everything for 7 mins.
- Add in the rice and toast the kernels for 2 mins then add in the tomato sauce and broth.
- Get the mix boiling, set the heat to a low level, and simmer everything for 22 mins.
- Stuff your peppers with the rice mix then place everything into the casserole dish.
- Cook the peppers in the oven for 17 mins.
- Enjoy.

Amount per serving (6 total)

Timing Information:

Preparation	45 m
Cooking	15 m
Total Time	1 h

Nutritional Information:

Calories	307 kcal
Fat	9.6 g
Carbohydrates	39.9g
Protein	17 g
Cholesterol	90 mg
Sodium	954 mg

* Percent Daily Values are based on a 2,000 calorie diet.

Creole Soup

Ingredients

- 1/2 C. unsalted butter
- 1 onion, chopped
- 2 cloves garlic, diced
- 1/4 C. all-purpose flour
- 2 C. clam juice
- 2 C. chicken broth
- 1 (10 oz.) package frozen white corn
- 1 tsp salt
- 1/2 tsp ground white pepper
- 1/4 tsp dried thyme
- 1/4 tsp ground cayenne pepper
- 2 C. heavy cream
- 1 lb lump crabmeat, drained
- 4 green onions, chopped

Directions

- Begin to stir fry your garlic and onions, in butter, until the onions are soft then add in the flour. Stir and cook the mix for 3 mins then add the broth and clam liquid. Get everything boiling then add the cayenne, corn, thyme, salt, and white pepper.
- Stir the mix again then set the heat to low.
- Let everything cook for 17 mins.
- Now add in the green onions, crab, and cream.
- Stir everything again and get it all hot. Enjoy.

Amount per serving (8 total)

Timing Information:

Preparation	15 m
Cooking	30 m
Total Time	45 m

Nutritional Information:

Calories	420 kcal
Fat	34.6 g
Carbohydrates	14.5g
Protein	15.1 g
Cholesterol	164 mg
Sodium	636 mg

* Percent Daily Values are based on a 2,000 calorie diet.

Hannah's Jambalaya

Ingredients

- 2 tbsps peanut oil, divided
- 1 tbsp Cajun seasoning
- 10 oz. andouille sausage, sliced into rounds
- 1 lb boneless skinless chicken breasts, cut into 1 inch pieces
- 1 onion, diced
- 1 small green bell pepper, diced
- 2 stalks celery, diced
- 3 cloves garlic, diced
- 1 (16 oz.) can crushed Italian tomatoes
- 1/2 tsp red pepper flakes
- 1/2 tsp ground black pepper
- 1 tsp salt
- 1/2 tsp hot pepper sauce
- 2 tsps Worcestershire sauce
- 1 tsp file powder
- 1 1/4 C. uncooked white rice
- 2 1/2 C. chicken broth

Directions

- Coat your chicken and sausage with the Cajun spice and fry the sausage in 1 tbsp of peanut oil until everything is browned then remove it from the pan.
- Pour in another tbsp of peanut oil and begin to brown your chicken on all sides. Then place the chicken to the side as well.

- Begin to stir fry your garlic, onions, celery, and bell peppers until the onions are soft then add in the file powder, red pepper, Worcestershire, black pepper, hot sauce, and salt.
- Stir the spices then add in the crushed tomatoes.
- Stir the mix again then add in the sausage and chicken.
- Let the mix cook for 13 mins then add the broth and the rice as well.
- Get the mix boiling, set the heat to low, and let the contents cook for 22 mins.
- Enjoy.

Amount per serving (6 total)

Timing Information:

Preparation	20 m
Cooking	45 m
Total Time	1 h 5 m

Nutritional Information:

Calories	465 kcal
Fat	19.8 g
Carbohydrates	42.4g
Protein	28.1 g
Cholesterol	73 mg
Sodium	1633 mg

* Percent Daily Values are based on a 2,000 calorie diet.

Cajun Burger

Ingredients

- 1/2 C. mayonnaise
- 1 tsp Cajun seasoning
- 1 1/3 lbs ground beef sirloin
- 1 jalapeno pepper, seeded and chopped
- 1/2 C. diced white onion
- 1 clove garlic, diced
- 1 tbsp Cajun seasoning
- 1 tsp Worcestershire sauce
- 4 slices pepperjack cheese
- 4 hamburger buns, split
- 4 leaves lettuce
- 4 slices tomato

Directions

- Get your outdoor grill hot and coat the grate with oil.
- Get a bowl, combine: 1 tsp Cajun seasoning and mayo.
- Stir the mix until it is smooth. Get a 2nd bowl, combine: Worcestershire, sirloin, 1 tbsp Cajun spice, jalapeno, garlic, and the onions. Combine the mix with your hands then shape everything into 4 burgers. Grill the burgers for 6 mins each side.
- Lay a piece of pepper jack on each patty and let the cheese melt. Then place the burgers to the side.
- Coat your bread with the mayo mix then lay your patties, some tomato, and lettuce, on each one. Enjoy.

Amount per serving (4 total)

Timing Information:

Preparation	25 m
Cooking	15 m
Total Time	40 m

Nutritional Information:

Calories	714 kcal
Fat	49.1 g
Carbohydrates	28.5g
Protein	38.3 g
Cholesterol	132 mg
Sodium	1140 mg

* Percent Daily Values are based on a 2,000 calorie diet.

Cajun Pulled Pork

Ingredients

- 1 tbsp butter
- 2 lbs boneless pork roast
- 1 tbsp Cajun seasoning
- 1 medium onion, chopped
- 4 cloves garlic, crushed
- 4 C. water
- 1 tbsp liquid smoke flavoring

Directions

- Coat your pork with the Cajun spice and sear the meat in butter.
- Now place it in the crock of a slow cooker.
- Begin to fry your garlic and onions in the same pan for 3 mins then add in the water and scrape the pan.
- Pour everything over the pork. Then add the liquid smoke and place the lid on the slow cooker.
- Let the pork cook for 6 hours with a high level of heat. Then shred the meat.
- Enjoy.

Amount per serving (6 total)

Timing Information:

Preparation	30 m
Cooking	6 h
Total Time	6 h 30 m

Nutritional Information:

Calories	178 kcal
Fat	10.1 g
Carbohydrates	2.9g
Protein	< 17.9 g
Cholesterol	58 mg
Sodium	282 mg

* Percent Daily Values are based on a 2,000 calorie diet.

Cajun Pretzel

Ingredients

- 1 (16 oz.) package mini sourdough pretzels
- 1 C. Corn Oil
- 1 (1 oz.) packet ranch dressing mix
- 1 tbsp Cajun seasoning
- 1 tsp Cayenne Pepper
- 1 tsp Dried Dill Weed

Directions

- Set your oven to 200 degrees before doing anything else.
- Layer your pieces of pretzel in a casserole dish then get a bowl and combine: the dill, corn oil, cayenne, ranch dressing mix, and Cajun spice.
- Top your pieces of pretzels with this mix.
- Then cook everything in the oven for 2 hrs.
- Stir the pretzels every 20 mins.
- Enjoy.

Amount per serving (10 total)

Timing Information:

Preparation	10 m
Cooking	2 h
Total Time	2 h 10 m

Nutritional Information:

Calories	384 kcal
Fat	22.5 g
Carbohydrates	39.8g
Protein	4.6 g
Cholesterol	0 mg
Sodium	641 mg

* Percent Daily Values are based on a 2,000 calorie diet.

Cajun Breakfast

Ingredients

- 1 tbsp butter
- 1 egg
- 1 slice Cheddar cheese
- 1 tsp mayonnaise, or to taste
- 1 tsp mustard, or to taste
- 1 tsp ketchup, or to taste
- 1 pinch Cajun seasoning
- 1 dash hot pepper sauce
- 2 slices white bread, toasted
- 1 lettuce leaf
- 1 slice tomato

Directions

- Get your butter hot in a frying pan then break the egg directly into the pan.
- Let the egg fry until the whites set then turn the egg over and fry it for 4 mins.
- Lay a piece of cheddar over the egg and let it melt for 1 to 2 mins.
- Coat your pieces of bread with: ketchup, mustard, and mayo.
- Then top the egg with some Cajun spice. Place the tomato and lettuce on a piece of bread then lay the egg on the other.
- Add some hot sauce to your egg and also any butter in the pan.
- Form a sandwich between the two pieces of bread. Enjoy.

Amount per serving (1 total)

Timing Information:

Preparation	10 m
Cooking	5 m
Total Time	15 m

Nutritional Information:

Calories	471 kcal
Fat	31.5 g
Carbohydrates	29.6g
Protein	18.1 g
Cholesterol	248 mg
Sodium	996 mg

* Percent Daily Values are based on a 2,000 calorie diet.

Creole Corn

Ingredients

- 1 sheet (12-inch square) pieces aluminum foil
- 1 (10 oz.) package frozen whole kernel corn
- 1 small onion, chopped
- 1 C. chopped tomatoes
- 3/4 C. chopped green bell pepper
- 2 tsps creole seasoning
- 1 tbsp margarine or butter

Directions

- Set your oven to 450 degrees before doing anything else.
- Lay out a piece of foil and place your veggies in the middle.
- Top the veggies with the creole spice and toss them to evenly distribute the spices.
- Now coat the veggies with margarine and shape the foil into a packet with spice in the middle.
- Place the veggies in the oven for 22 mins.
- Enjoy.

Amount per serving (4 total)

Timing Information:

Preparation	
Cooking	25 m
Total Time	25 m

Nutritional Information:

Calories	110 kcal
Fat	3.4 g
Carbohydrates	20.1g
Protein	3.1 g
Cholesterol	0 mg
Sodium	274 mg

* Percent Daily Values are based on a 2,000 calorie diet.

Creole Fried Snapper

Ingredients

- 1 1/2 C. dry bread crumbs
- 1 1/2 tsps creole seasoning
- salt to taste
- 2 eggs
- 1 C. buttermilk
- 1 1/2 lbs red snapper fillets, bones removed
- 1 C. flour
- vegetable oil as needed

Directions

- Get a bowl, combine: salt, creole spice, and bread crumbs.
- Get a 2nd bowl, combine: buttermilk, and eggs.
- Coat your fish with flour first then with eggs and finally with the bread crumbs.
- Get 1/4 of a C. of oil hot and then fry your fish for 4 mins each side.
- Enjoy.

Amount per serving (4 total)

Timing Information:

Preparation	10 m
Cooking	6 m
Total Time	16 m

Nutritional Information:

Calories	627 kcal
Fat	21.4 g
Carbohydrates	56.6g
Protein	48.9 g
Cholesterol	158 mg
Sodium	795 mg

* Percent Daily Values are based on a 2,000 calorie diet.

Creole Fried Catfish

Ingredients

- 2 lbs catfish fillets, cut into 2 inch pieces
- 1 C. milk, or as needed
- 1 egg
- 1/4 C. all-purpose flour
- 1/4 C. cornmeal
- 2 tsps ground black pepper
- 2 tsps ground mustard
- 2 tbsps creole seasoning
- 1 dash pepper sauce
- 1/4 C. oil for frying, or as needed

Directions

- Let your fish sit submerged in milk for 40 mins.
- Get a bowl, combine: hot sauce and eggs.
- Get a 2nd bowl, combine: creole spice, flour, mustard, cornmeal, and pepper.
- Coat your fish with the creole spice mix, then the egg mix, and finally the spice mix again.
- Place the pieces of fish in a casserole dish and place a covering of plastic over everything. Place the casserole dish in the fridge for 30 mins.
- Get your oil hot in a frying pan then cook your fish for 5 mins each side.
- Enjoy.

Amount per serving (4 total)

Timing Information:

Preparation	10 m
Cooking	15 m
Total Time	1 h 10 m

Nutritional Information:

Calories	448 kcal
Fat	22 g
Carbohydrates	18.4g
Protein	41.2 g
Cholesterol	158 mg
Sodium	877 mg

* Percent Daily Values are based on a 2,000 calorie diet.

Louisiana Chowder

Ingredients

- 1 (16 oz.) package mixed frozen vegetables
- 2 tbsps butter
- 3/4 C. chopped onion
- 1 clove garlic, diced
- 1 (4 oz.) package sliced fresh mushrooms
- 1 tbsp Cajun seasoning
- 2 tbsps all-purpose flour
- 1 1/2 C. milk
- 1 lb scallops, cleaned and cut in half
- 1 tsp salt
- 1/8 tsp ground black pepper

Directions

- Get your veggies boiling in after for 10 mins. Then remove the liquids.
- Begin to stir fry your mushrooms, onions, garlic, and Cajun spice, in butter for 7 mins.
- Now add in your flour and stir the mix.
- Add the milk and stir everything again and let the mix being to simmer and get thick.
- Combine in the pepper, salt, and scallops and let the mix cook for 9 mins then add the veggie mix to the pan and stir everything for 4 mins.
- Enjoy.

Amount per serving (4 total)

Timing Information:

Preparation	10 m
Cooking	20 m
Total Time	30 m

Nutritional Information:

Calories	355 kcal
Fat	9.5 g
Carbohydrates	32.7g
Protein	37.1 g
Cholesterol	91 mg
Sodium	1398 mg

* Percent Daily Values are based on a 2,000 calorie diet.

French Quarter Mushrooms

Ingredients

- 1 (8 oz.) package cream cheese, softened
- 1/2 C. shredded Colby-Monterey Jack cheese
- 1 tsp seafood seasoning
- 1/2 tsp Cajun seasoning
- 1/4 tsp cayenne hot pepper sauce, or to taste
- 1/4 tsp garlic powder
- 1 (8 oz.) package imitation crabmeat, flaked
- 1/4 C. Italian seasoned bread crumbs
- 1 (8 oz.) package crimini mushrooms, stems removed

Directions

- Coat a casserole dish with oil then set your oven to 350 degrees before doing anything else.
- Get a bowl, combine: garlic powder, cream cheese, hot sauce, Colby jack, Cajun spice, and seafood seasoning.
- Stir the mix evenly then add in the bread crumbs and the crab.
- Stir the mix again and stuff your mushrooms with it.
- Place the mushrooms in the casserole dish and cook them in the oven for 20 mins then place the mushrooms under the broiler for 4 mins.
- Enjoy.

Amount per serving (4 total)

Timing Information:

Preparation	20 m
Cooking	10 m
Total Time	30 m

Nutritional Information:

Calories	364 kcal
Fat	25.7 g
Carbohydrates	17.9g
Protein	15.9 g
Cholesterol	89 mg
Sodium	1124 mg

* Percent Daily Values are based on a 2,000 calorie diet.

Cajun Burger II

Ingredients

- 1 lb ground beef
- 3 tbsps dry bread crumbs
- 1 egg
- 3 green onions, chopped
- 1 tbsp Cajun seasoning
- 1 tbsp prepared mustard
- 1/4 C. barbeque sauce
- 1 tsp Cajun seasoning
- 4 slices Cheddar cheese

Directions

- Get a bowl, combine: mustard, beef, 1 tbsp Cajun spice, bread crumbs, green onions, and egg.
- Shape the mix into 4 burgers.
- Get a 2nd bowl, combine: 1 tsp Cajun spice and bbq sauce.
- Get your grill hot and coat the grate with oil.
- Cook the burgers for 6 mins each side then lay a piece of cheese over the patties.
- Let the cheese melt then top your burgers with the bbq sauce.
- Enjoy.

Amount per serving (4 total)

Timing Information:

Preparation	10 m
Cooking	20 m
Total Time	30 m

Nutritional Information:

Calories	414 kcal
Fat	27.4 g
Carbohydrates	11.9g
Protein	28.7 g
Cholesterol	147 mg
Sodium	989 mg

* Percent Daily Values are based on a 2,000 calorie diet.

Bayou Blue Salad

Ingredients

- 1/4 C. mayonnaise
- 1/8 C. prepared mustard
- 4 tsps sweet relish
- 2 (16 oz.) cans pineapple chunks
- 1 tsp Cajun pepper
- 2 lbs iceberg lettuce, shredded
- 1 C. bay leaves

Directions

- Get a bowl, combine: relish, mayo, and mustard. Stir everything until it is smooth and even.
- Get a 2nd bowl, combine: Cajun pepper and pineapple.
- Add your lettuce to a 3rd bowl for serving then add the pineapple mix and add the mustard mix.
- Toss everything completely.
- Enjoy.

Amount per serving (10 total)

Timing Information:

Preparation	
Cooking	15 m
Total Time	15 m

Nutritional Information:

Calories	121 kcal
Fat	5 g
Carbohydrates	20.3g
Protein	1.6 g
Cholesterol	2 mg
Sodium	< 141 mg

* Percent Daily Values are based on a 2,000 calorie diet.

Mardi-Gras Potatoes

Ingredients

- 4 baking potatoes
- 3 tbsps olive oil
- 1 tsp diced fresh garlic
- 1/4 tsp salt
- 1/4 tsp ground black pepper
- 1 1/2 tsps onion powder
- 1/2 tsp paprika

Directions

- Coat a casserole dish with oil then set your oven to 425 degrees before doing anything else.
- Slice your potatoes into 12 pieces then add them to a bowl.
- Combine with the potatoes: the paprika, olive oil, onion powder, garlic, pepper, and salt.
- Place the slices in the casserole dish and cook them in the oven for 22 mins.
- Flip everything then continue cooking the mix for 27 more mins.
- Enjoy.

Amount per serving (4 total)

Timing Information:

Preparation	10 m
Cooking	45 m
Total Time	55 m

Nutritional Information:

Calories	258 kcal
Fat	10.4 g
Carbohydrates	38.3g
Protein	4.5 g
Cholesterol	0 mg
Sodium	159 mg

* Percent Daily Values are based on a 2,000 calorie diet.

Creole Fries

Ingredients

- 2 lbs russet potatoes, cut into fries
- 1 C. corn flour
- 2 tbsps cornmeal
- 2 tbsps creole seasoning
- 1 quart oil for deep frying
- salt to taste

Directions

- Let your potatoes sit submerged in water for 12 mins then add the following to a resealable bag: creole seasoning, corn flour, and corn meal.
- Combine the spices then add the potatoes to the bag with a slotted spoon or with your hands.
- Coat the potatoes evenly with the mix.
- Deep fry the potatoes for 9 mins in oil then top everything with some more salt before serving.
- Enjoy.

Amount per serving (6 total)

Timing Information:

Preparation	20 m
Cooking	10 m
Total Time	30 m

Nutritional Information:

Calories	342 kcal
Fat	15.3 g
Carbohydrates	47.3g
Protein	4.6 g
Cholesterol	0 mg
Sodium	548 mg

* Percent Daily Values are based on a 2,000 calorie diet.

Cajun Mushrooms and Broccoli

Ingredients

- 1 (10 oz.) package frozen chopped broccoli, thawed
- 1 C. fresh green beans, trimmed
- 2 tbsps butter
- 1 C. sliced fresh mushrooms
- 1 (15 oz.) can baby corn, drained
- 1 tbsp Cajun seasoning
- 1 tbsp olive oil

Directions

- Get your green beans and broccoli boiling in water.
- Let the veggies cook for 7 mins then remove all of the liquids.
- Begin to stir fry your mushrooms in butter for 2 mins then combine in the corn and cook it for 2 more mins.
- Add the beans and mushrooms then top everything with the olive oil and Cajun spice.
- Enjoy.

Amount per serving (6 total)

Timing Information:

Preparation	10 m
Cooking	10 m
Total Time	20 m

Nutritional Information:

Calories	90 kcal
Fat	6.3 g
Carbohydrates	7g
Protein	2.2 g
Cholesterol	10 mg
Sodium	302 mg

* Percent Daily Values are based on a 2,000 calorie diet.

Creole Cabbage

Ingredients

- 1 tsp chili powder
- 1 tsp dried thyme
- 1 tsp smoked paprika
- 1 tsp dried oregano
- 1/2 tsp ground cayenne pepper
- 1/2 tsp ground cumin
- 1/2 tsp onion powder
- 1 tsp salt
- 2 tbsps butter
- 1 small onion, sliced
- 3 cloves garlic, diced
- 1 small head cabbage, finely shredded

Directions

- Get a bowl, combine: salt, chili powder, onion powder, thyme, cumin, paprika, cayenne, and oregano.
- Begin to stir fry your onions in butter for 7 mins then stir in the garlic and cook it for 3 more mins.
- Now combine in the cabbage and cook the leaves for 7 mins.
- Then add the spices to the cabbage and stir the mix for 5 more mins.
- Enjoy.

Amount per serving (4 total)

Timing Information:

Preparation	15 m
Cooking	15 m
Total Time	30 m

Nutritional Information:

Calories	114 kcal
Fat	6.3 g
Carbohydrates	14.3g
Protein	3 g
Cholesterol	15 mg
Sodium	663 mg

* Percent Daily Values are based on a 2,000 calorie diet.

Creole Cauliflower

Ingredients

- cooking spray
- 1 large head cauliflower, cut into small florets
- 2 tbsps olive oil, or as needed
- 1 tbsp creole seasoning
- 1 tbsp garlic salt
- 1 tsp salt

Directions

- Coat a casserole dish with nonstick spray then set your oven to 500 degrees before doing anything else.
- Get a bowl, combine: garlic salt, olive oil, and creole spice.
- Stir the mix until it is smooth then add in your cauliflower.
- Toss the florets to cover them with the spices and oil then pour everything into the casserole dish.
- Top the veggies with some salt then place a covering of foil around the dish.
- Cook everything in the oven for 13 mins.
- Take off the foil, flip the florets, and continue cooking the veggies for 16 more mins.
- Enjoy.

Amount per serving (4 total)

Timing Information:

Preparation	10 m
Cooking	25 m
Total Time	35 m

Nutritional Information:

Calories	120 kcal
Fat	7.1 g
Carbohydrates	12.4g
Protein	4.4 g
Cholesterol	0 mg
Sodium	2359 mg

* Percent Daily Values are based on a 2,000 calorie diet.

Bayou Andouille Rice

Ingredients

- 1 C. uncooked wild rice
- 1 (14 oz.) can chicken broth
- 1/4 C. water
- 1/2 lb andouille sausage, diced
- 1/2 C. diced sweet onion
- 1 C. chopped fresh mushrooms
- 1 tbsp diced garlic
- 1 (10.75 oz.) can condensed cream of mushroom soup

Directions

- Get the following boiling: garlic, rice, mushrooms, broth, onion, sausage, and water.
- Set the heat to low, place a lid on the pot, and let the mix cook for 27 mins.
- Now shut the heat and add in your mushroom soup.
- Stir the soup into the rice so that it is evenly distributed.
- Enjoy.

Amount per serving (6 total)

Timing Information:

Preparation	10 m
Cooking	45 m
Total Time	55 m

Nutritional Information:

Calories	248 kcal
Fat	14.3 g
Carbohydrates	21.2g
Protein	9.1 g
Cholesterol	24 mg
Sodium	989 mg

* Percent Daily Values are based on a 2,000 calorie diet.

Crossroads Beef

Ingredients

- 2 tsps garlic, diced
- 1/2 tsp prepared horseradish
- 1 tsp hot pepper sauce
- 1 tsp dried thyme
- 1/2 tsp salt
- 1/2 tsp ground black pepper
- 2 tsps Cajun seasoning
- 2 tbsps olive oil
- 2 tbsps malt vinegar
- 2 lbs beef eye of round roast

Directions

- Get a bowl, combine: malt vinegar, garlic, olive oil, horseradish, Cajun spice, hot sauce, pepper, salt, and thyme.
- Perforate the beef with a large fork then place the beef in a big plastic bag that can be sealed.
- Add in the oil mix and coat the meat evenly. Squeeze out any excess air in the bag then place the meat in the fridge for 8 hrs.
- Add the meat to the crock pot of a slow cooker and the marinade as well.
- Place the lid on the slow cooker and cook the meat for 9 hrs with low level of heat.
- Enjoy.

Amount per serving (8 total)

Timing Information:

Preparation	15 m
Cooking	8 h
Total Time	16 h 15 m

Nutritional Information:

Calories	148 kcal
Fat	9.7 g
Carbohydrates	1.1g
Protein	< 13.4 g
Cholesterol	36 mg
Sodium	311 mg

* Percent Daily Values are based on a 2,000 calorie diet.

Cajun County Stuffing

Ingredients

- 5 quarts chicken broth
- 10 C. uncooked white rice
- 1 1/2 C. chopped celery
- 1 1/2 C. chopped onion, divided
- 1 tbsp garlic, diced
- 1 lb bulk pork sausage
- 1 lb ground beef
- 1 tbsp dried thyme
- 1 tbsp dried parsley
- 1 tbsp dried oregano

Directions

- Get the following boiling in a large pot: 1 C. chopped onion, broth, celery, and rice.
- Once the mix is boiling, set the heat to low, place a lid on the pot, and let the mix cook for 22 mins.
- At the same time begin to fry your beef, 1/2 C. of onions, sausage, and garlic.
- Once the meat is fully done remove the oils from the pan then combine the mix with the rice once the rice is finished cooking.
- Stir everything together then add in your oregano, thyme, and parsley.
- Enjoy.

Amount per serving (20 total)

Timing Information:

Preparation	15 m
Cooking	30 m
Total Time	45 m

Nutritional Information:

Calories	445 kcal
Fat	8.3 g
Carbohydrates	76g
Protein	13.8 g
Cholesterol	27 mg
Sodium	228 mg

* Percent Daily Values are based on a 2,000 calorie diet.

Louisiana Popcorn

Ingredients

- 20 C. popped popcorn
- 1/2 C. butter or margarine, melted
- 2 tsps paprika
- 2 tsps lemon pepper
- 1 tsp salt
- 1 tsp garlic powder
- 1 tsp onion powder
- 1/4 tsp cayenne pepper

Directions

- Set your oven to 350 degrees before doing anything else.
- Get a bowl, combine cayenne, melted butter, onion powder, paprika, garlic powder, salt, and lemon pepper.
- Stir the mix until it is smooth then add your popcorn to a casserole dish.
- Top the popcorn with the butter mix and toss everything.
- Cook the popcorn for 20 mins in the oven and toss the kernels 4 times as they cook.
- Enjoy.

Amount per serving (20 total)

Timing Information:

Preparation	15 m
Cooking	15 m
Total Time	30 m

Nutritional Information:

Calories	107 kcal
Fat	9.4 g
Carbohydrates	5.3g
Protein	0.9 g
Cholesterol	12 mg
Sodium	312 mg

* Percent Daily Values are based on a 2,000 calorie diet.

Cajun Country Dough

Ingredients

- 3/4 C. unsalted butter, softened
- 1 1/3 C. white sugar
- 1 tsp vanilla extract
- 1 egg
- 4 1/2 C. all-purpose flour
- 2 tsps baking powder
- 1 tsp salt
- 1/2 C. milk
- 1 (12.5 oz.) can cherry pie filling
- 1 egg white (for egg wash)

Directions

- Get a bowl, combine: salt, baking powder, and flour.
- Get a 2nd bowl, combine: sugar and butter.
- Combine the mix evenly then add in the vanilla.
- Whisk the mix until it is fluffy then add the egg and continue mixing everything.
- Now add your milk and flour gradually and form a dough from the mix.
- Place a covering of plastic on the bowl and put everything in the fridge for 3 hrs.
- Now set your oven to 350 degrees before doing anything else.
- Knead your dough into a large sheet that is a quarter of an inch thick.

- Slice the dough in small squares and place 2 tbsps of cherry filling in the middle of each square.
- Shape the dough into a triangle and crimp the edges with a fork.
- Lay everything into a casserole dish coated with oil and brush them with egg whites.
- Cook the turnovers in the oven for 13 mins.
- Enjoy.

Amount per serving (30 total)

Timing Information:

Preparation	
Cooking	15 m
Total Time	15 m

Nutritional Information:

Calories	162 kcal
Fat	5 g
Carbohydrates	26.8g
Protein	2.5 g
Cholesterol	19 mg
Sodium	119 mg

* Percent Daily Values are based on a 2,000 calorie diet.

Greater New Orleans Stew

Ingredients

- nonstick cooking spray
- 1 onion, thinly sliced
- 1 green bell pepper, cut into strips
- 1 red bell pepper, cut into strips
- 2 C. fresh okra, cut into 1/2 inch slices
- 1 whole boneless, skinless chicken breast, cubed
- 1 tbsp Cajun seasoning
- 1 lb whole cooked crawfish, peeled
- 1/4 C. butter
- 2 tbsps all-purpose flour
- 3 C. milk
- 1/3 C. half-and-half cream
- 1 pinch salt
- 3 C. shredded Cheddar cheese
- 1 C. freshly grated Romano cheese
- 1/3 C. chili powder
- 1 tbsp ground paprika

Directions

- Stir fry your okra, bell peppers, and onions in a pan coated with nonstick spray until everything is soft. Then add in some Cajun spice.
- Remove the veggies from the pan.

- Coat the pan again with cooking spray and begin to fry your chicken until it is fully done then add in 1 tbsp of Cajun spice.
- Evenly coat the meat with the spice then add in the crawfish and cook them for 2 more mins.
- Now take everything out of the pot and add in your butter.
- Get the butter melted then add in your flour and begin to stir the mix until everything is bubbling.
- Combine in the milk and begin to stir it as you pour in the half and half and keep stirring.
- Once the mix is smooth and thick add some salt, and the cheddar slowly.
- Let the cheese melt then combine in the Romano.
- Stir the Romano into the sauce then add the paprika and chili powder.
- Combine the spices in evenly then add the veggie mix, crawfish and chicken.
- Let the entire mix cook for 7 mins, while stirring, then shut the heat and leave the dish for 10 mins.
- Enjoy.

Amount per serving (6 total)

Timing Information:

Preparation	20 m
Cooking	40 m
Total Time	1 h

Nutritional Information:

Calories	614 kcal
Fat	38.5 g
Carbohydrates	21g
Protein	47.8 g
Cholesterol	219 mg
Sodium	1085 mg

* Percent Daily Values are based on a 2,000 calorie diet.

Southern Louisiana Vegetable Medley (Maque Choux)

Ingredients

- 6 ears corn, husked and cleaned
- 2 tbsps vegetable oil
- 1 large onion, thinly sliced
- 1 C. green bell pepper, chopped
- 1 large fresh tomato, chopped
- 1/4 C. milk
- salt to taste
- cayenne pepper
- 1/4 C. chopped green onions
- 8 strips crisply cooked bacon, crumbled

Directions

- Get a bowl.
- With a sharp knife, safely slice the kernels of corn off of the cob. Add the milk to the bowl and stir everything.
- Begin to stir fry your green pepper and onions, in oil, for 7 mins, then add in the tomatoes and corn.
- Set the heat to low and let the mix cook for 25 mins.
- Stir the mix every 5 mins but avoid boiling it.
- Then add in the cayenne and salt.

- Stir the spices in evenly then set the heat lower, place a lid on the pan, and continue cooking everything for 7 more mins.
- Now add your bacon and the green onions.
- Enjoy.

Amount per serving (6 total)

Timing Information:

Preparation	35 m
Cooking	30 m
Total Time	1 h 5 m

Nutritional Information:

Calories	211 kcal
Fat	11.1 g
Carbohydrates	22.8g
Protein	8.6 g
Cholesterol	14 mg
Sodium	371 mg

* Percent Daily Values are based on a 2,000 calorie diet.

Cajun Seeds

Ingredients

- 1 C. raw whole pumpkin seeds, washed and dried
- 1 tsp paprika (optional)
- 3/4 tsp Cajun seasoning, or to taste
- salt to taste
- 2 dashes Worcestershire sauce
- 1 tbsp butter, melted

Directions

- Set your oven to 300 degrees before doing anything else.
- Get a bowl, combine: salt, pumpkin seeds, Cajun spice, and paprika.
- Get a 2nd bowl, combine: melted butter and Worcestershire sauce.
- Stir everything until it is smooth then coat your pumpkin seeds with the mix.
- Lay your seeds into a casserole dish and cook them in the oven for 50 mins.
- Flip the seeds at least twice as they cook.
- Enjoy.

Amount per serving (5 total)

Timing Information:

Preparation	15 m
Cooking	45 m
Total Time	1 h

Nutritional Information:

Calories	80 kcal
Fat	4.9 g
Carbohydrates	7.3g
Protein	2.5 g
Cholesterol	6 mg
Sodium	169 mg

* Percent Daily Values are based on a 2,000 calorie diet.

Cajun Lasagna

Ingredients

- 1 (16 oz.) package lasagna noodles
- 1 lb andouille sausage, quartered lengthwise and sliced
- 1 lb skinless, boneless chicken breast halves, cut into chunks
- 2 tsps Cajun seasoning
- 1 tsp dried sage
- 1/2 C. chopped onion
- 1/2 C. chopped celery
- 1/4 C. chopped red bell pepper
- 1 tbsp finely chopped garlic
- 2 (10 oz.) containers Alfredo Sauce, divided
- 1 1/2 C. shredded mozzarella cheese
- 1/2 C. grated Parmesan cheese

Directions

- Set your oven to 325 degrees before doing anything else.
- Get your pasta boiling in water and salt for 9 mins then remove all the liquids.
- Begin to fry your chicken and sausage then top the meats with the sage and Cajun spice.
- Continue cooking the meat until the chicken is fully done for 10 mins.

- Place everything to the side then begin to stir fry your garlic, onions, bell peppers, and celery until everything is soft.
- Place these veggies to the side as well.
- Combine the meat and veggies together then add in 1 jar of Alfredo and stir everything evenly.
- Coat a casserole dish with oil then lay in 4 pieces of pasta.
- Top the pasta with half of the Alfredo mix.
- Continue layering in this manner until all the pasta has been added.
- Top the layers with the remaining jar of sauce then layer your parmesan and mozzarella over everything.
- Cook the lasagna in the oven for 60 mins.
- Enjoy.

Amount per serving (12 total)

Timing Information:

Preparation	15 m
Cooking	1 h 15 m
Total Time	1 h 45 m

Nutritional Information:

Calories	488 kcal
Fat	29 g
Carbohydrates	32g
Protein	25.4 g
Cholesterol	75 mg
Sodium	1045 mg

* Percent Daily Values are based on a 2,000 calorie diet.

Muffuletta (Louisiana Sandwich)

Ingredients

- 1 C. pimento-stuffed green olives, crushed
- 1/2 C. drained kalamata olives, crushed
- 2 cloves garlic, minced
- 1/4 C. roughly chopped pickled cauliflower florets
- 2 tbsps drained capers
- 1 tbsp chopped celery
- 1 tbsp chopped carrot
- 1/2 C. pepperoncini, drained
- 1/4 C. marinated cocktail onions
- 1/2 tsp celery seed
- 1 tsp dried oregano
- 1 tsp dried basil
- 3/4 tsp ground black pepper
- 1/4 C. red wine vinegar
- 1/2 C. olive oil
- 1/4 C. canola oil
- 2 (1 lb) loaves Italian bread
- 8 oz. thinly sliced Genoa salami
- 8 oz. thinly sliced cooked ham
- 8 oz. sliced mortadella
- 8 oz. sliced mozzarella cheese
- 8 oz. sliced provolone cheese

Directions

- Get a bowl, combine: all oils, all your olives, vinegar, garlic, black pepper, cauliflower, basil, capers, oregano, celery, celery seed, carrot, pepperoncini, and cocktail onions.
- Let the salad sit covered in the fridge for at least 6 to 8 hours.
- Dice your bread into two pieces horizontally.
- Remove some the insides of the bread to make more space.
- Top each piece with some salad.
- On the bottom part of your bread layer: cheese, salami, mortadella, and ham.
- Form your sandwich and cut it up into serving pieces.
- Chill the sandwiches before serving for 2 hours in the fridge.
- Enjoy.

Amount per serving (8 total)

Timing Information:

Preparation	
Cooking	40 m
Total Time	1 d 40 m

Nutritional Information:

Calories	987 kcal
Fat	62.8 g
Carbohydrates	63.2g
Protein	41.4 g
Cholesterol	97 mg
Sodium	3465 mg

* Percent Daily Values are based on a 2,000 calorie diet.

Creole Pasta II

Ingredients

- 6 tbsps butter
- 1 large onion, chopped
- 1 green bell pepper, chopped
- 3 stalks celery, chopped
- 1 clove garlic, minced
- 1 tbsp all-purpose flour
- 1 lb peeled crawfish tails
- 1 (8 oz.) package processed cheese food
- 1 C. half-and-half cream
- 2 tsps Cajun seasoning
- 1 pinch cayenne pepper, or to taste
- 1 lb dry fettuccine pasta
- 1/2 C. grated Parmesan cheese

Directions

- Fry the following in butter until soft: garlic, onions, celery, and bell pepper.
- Now add in your flour and stir for 9 mins.
- Add your crawfish and place a lid on the pan and lie the contents simmer for 17 mins.
- Combine the: cayenne, cheese, Cajun seasonings, and half and half.
- Set your oven to 350 degrees before doing anything else.

- Boil your pasta for 9 mins in water and salt. The remove all the liquid.
- Get a casserole dish and grease it with some butter. Then add your fish mix, and the noodles.
- Garnish everything with parmesan then cook the contents in the oven for 22 mins.
- Enjoy.

Amount per serving (8 total)

Timing Information:

Preparation	15 m
Cooking	1 h 15 m
Total Time	1 h 30 m

Nutritional Information:

Calories	490 kcal
Fat	22.6 g
Carbohydrates	48.9g
Protein	24 g
Cholesterol	122 mg
Sodium	682 mg

* Percent Daily Values are based on a 2,000 calorie diet.

Po' Boy

Ingredients

- Vegetable oil for deep-frying
- 4 French rolls, split and hinged
- 4 tbsps melted butter
- 1 tsp minced garlic
- 3 eggs, beaten
- 2 tbsps Creole seasoning
- 3/4 C. all-purpose flour
- 2 lbs jumbo shrimp, peeled and deveined
- 2 C. Kikkoman Panko Bread Crumbs
- 2 C. shredded lettuce
- Remoulade sauce:
- 1/2 C. mayonnaise
- 1 tbsp horseradish
- 1 tsp pickle relish
- 1 tsp minced garlic
- 1/2 tsp cayenne pepper
- 2 tbsps Kikkoman Ponzu Lime

Directions

- Coat your bread with garlic and butter before doing anything else.
- Coat your shrimp with flour and creole seasoning.
- Then dip it in some whisked eggs, and finally in panko.
- Now deep fry the shrimp in 360 degree hot oil.

- Now get a bowl and mix: ponzu lime, mayo, cayenne, relish, and minced garlic to together evenly.
- Coat your bread with a nice amount of this mix on each side.
- Then top the coated bread with your deep fried shrimp and some lettuce.
- Enjoy.

Amount per serving (4 total)

Timing Information:

Preparation	10 m
Cooking	1 h
Total Time	1 h 10 m

Nutritional Information:

Calories	1257 kcal
Fat	50 g
Carbohydrates	127.3g
Protein	73.2 g
Cholesterol	1526 mg
Sodium	12641 mg

* Percent Daily Values are based on a 2,000 calorie diet.

Jambalaya V

Ingredients

- 2 tbsps margarine or butter
- 1/4 C. chopped onion
- 1/3 C. chopped celery
- 1/4 C. chopped green pepper
- 1 (14.5 oz.) can diced tomatoes
- 1 1/2 C. chicken broth
- 2/3 C. long grain white rice
- 1 tsp dried basil
- 1/4 tsp garlic powder
- 1/4 tsp black pepper
- 1/4 tsp hot sauce
- 1 bay leaf
- 2/3 C. diced cooked chicken breast
- 2/3 C. cooked crumbled Italian sausage
- 2/3 C. peeled cooked shrimp

Directions

- Fry your green peppers, onions, and celery for 7 mins until tender. Then add broth, bay leaf, tomatoes, basil, house sauce, pepper, and garlic, and rice. Get this mix boiling and then lower the heat.
- Place a lid on the pot and let the rice cook for 22 mins.
- Now add your shrimp, chicken and sausage and let everything simmer for 4 more mins.
- Take out the bay leaf and then serve. Enjoy.

Amount per serving (4 total)

Timing Information:

Preparation	30 m
Cooking	30 m
Total Time	1 h

Nutritional Information:

Calories	369 kcal
Fat	16.6 g
Carbohydrates	31.5g
Protein	20.7 g
Cholesterol	78 mg
Sodium	704 mg

* Percent Daily Values are based on a 2,000 calorie diet.

Bourbon Chicken II

Ingredients

- 4 tbsps olive oil
- 3 lbs skinless, boneless chicken breast halves - cut into 1 inch pieces
- 1 C. water
- 1 C. packed light brown sugar
- 3/4 C. apple-grape-cherry juice
- 2/3 C. soy sauce
- 1/4 C. ketchup
- 1/4 C. peach-flavored bourbon liqueur
- 2 tbsps apple cider vinegar
- 2 cloves garlic, minced
- 1 tbsp dried minced onion
- 3/4 tsp crushed red pepper flakes, or to taste
- 1/2 tsp ground ginger
- 1/4 C. apple-grape-cherry juice
- 2 tbsps cornstarch

Directions

- Fry your chicken in a Dutch oven for 10 mins constantly stirring. Then place the chicken aside.
- Now add to the pot: ginger, water, red pepper, brown sugar, dried onion, 3/4 C. of fruit cocktail juice, garlic, soy sauce, vinegar, ketchup, and bourbon.

- Get this mix boiling and then add the chicken back in.
- Once everything is boiling again set the heat to low and simmer the mix until everything is thick for 20 mins.
- Take out the chicken again and place it aside with slotted spoon.
- Combine 1/4 C. fruit cocktail juice and cornstarch and then mix it with the sauce.
- Get the sauce boiling again for about 2 mins.
- Then add the chicken back to the mix and heat it through.
- Enjoy with rice.

Amount per serving (8 total)

Timing Information:

Preparation	15 m
Cooking	45 m
Total Time	1 h

Nutritional Information:

Calories	417 kcal
Fat	10.9 g
Carbohydrates	36.7g
Protein	37.1 g
Cholesterol	97 mg
Sodium	1382 mg

* Percent Daily Values are based on a 2,000 calorie diet.

Thanks for Reading! Now Let's Try some Sushi and Dump Dinners....

http://bit.ly/2443TFg

To grab this **box set** simply follow the link mentioned above, or tap the book cover.

This will take you to a page where you can simply enter your email address and a PDF version of the **box set** will be emailed to you.

I hope you are ready for some serious cooking!

http://bit.ly/2443TFg

You will also receive updates about all my new books when they are free.

Also don't forget to like and subscribe on the social networks. I love meeting my readers. Links to all my profiles are below so please click and connect :)

Facebook

Twitter

Come On...
Let's Be Friends :)

I adore my readers and love connecting with them socially. Please follow the links below so we can connect on Facebook, Twitter, and Google+.

Facebook

Twitter

I also have a blog that I regularly update for my readers so check it out below.

My Blog

Can I Ask A Favour?

If you found this book interesting, or have otherwise found any benefit in it. Then may I ask that you post a review of it on Amazon? Nothing excites me more than new reviews, especially reviews which suggest new topics for writing. I do read all reviews and I always factor feedback into my newer works.

So if you are willing to take ten minutes to write what you sincerely thought about this book then please visit our Amazon page and post your opinions.

Again thank you!

INTERESTED IN OTHER EASY COOKBOOKS?

Everything is easy! Check out my Amazon Author page for more great cookbooks:

For a complete listing of all my books please see my author page.

Made in the USA
San Bernardino, CA
31 May 2017